CHRISTMAS PROGRAMS FOR CHILDREN

Compiled by
Christine Spence

Standard
PUBLISHING
Bringing The Word to Life™

Cincinnati, Ohio

Standard Publishing
Cincinnati, Ohio.
A division of Standex International Corporation
© 2005 by Standard Publishing

ISBN 0-7847-1612-9

Contents

Christmas Songs

Jesus Christ Was Born
(Tune: "I Will Make You
Fishers of Men")
by Mary Tucker

Long ago in Bethlehem town,
    Bethlehem town, Bethlehem,
Long ago in Bethlehem town
    Jesus Christ was born.
Jesus Christ was born
That first Christmas morn.
Long ago in Bethlehem town Jesus Christ was born.

Angels told some shepherds nearby, shepherds nearby,
    shepherds nearby.
Angels told some shepherds nearby, "God has sent His Son."
"God has sent His Son.
He's the holy one."
Angels told some shepherds nearby, "God has sent His Son."

Shepherds went to worship the Lord, worship the Lord,
    worship the Lord.
Shepherds went to worship the Lord in His manger bed.
In His manger bed
As the angel said.
Shepherds went to worship the Lord in His manger bed.

A Happy Christmas Song
(Tune: "Pop Goes the Weasel")
by Mary Tucker

All around the sky that night the angel light was beaming.
Every shepherd said to himself, "Hey! I must be dreaming."

The angel said, "Do not be afraid. You're not in any danger.
Jesus Christ the Savior's been born. See Him in the manger."

All the shepherds hurried to town as fast as they were able
To find God's Son asleep in the hay. Where? In a cow stable.

Jesus, God's Son
(Tune: "This Old Man")
by Mary Tucker

Jesus Christ, God's own Son,
Came to earth for everyone.
In a stable lying in a manger bed,
Born just as the prophets said.

Jesus Christ came to be
God on earth with you and me.
When the shepherds saw Him sleeping in the stall,
They knew He was Lord of all.

Jesus came from above
To show us God's mighty love.
He would live and die so we could all be saved.
He's the truth, the life, the way.

A Merry Christmas
(Tune: "We Wish You a Merry Christmas")
by Mary Tucker

We wish you a merry Christmas.
We wish you a merry Christmas.
We wish you a merry Christmas
And a happy new year.

Did you know that Jesus loves you?
Did you know that Jesus loves you?
Did you know that Jesus loves you?
And He loves me too.

He came down to be your Savior.
He came down to be your Savior.
He came down to be your Savior.
Won't you give Him your heart?

Then you'll have a merry Christmas.
Then you'll have a merry Christmas.
Then you'll have a merry Christmas
And a happy new year!

Poems

Enjoy
by Dolores Steger

Enjoy each gift, each card, each toy.
But, then, with happiness and joy,
Shout praises for the Christ Child boy.

Born for You and Me
by Dolores Steger

Let every Christmas ornament
On every Christmas tree
Remind me of the Savior
Born for you and me.

Twinkle, Twinkle
by Dolores Steger

Twinkle, twinkle little star.
Shine on manger bed
Where the baby, Jesus, child
Rests His kingly head.

Happy Birthday
by Dolores Steger

Baby Jesus, little one,
We all know You are God's Son.
And on this, Your special day,
Happy Birthday's what we say!

Why?
by Dolores Steger

Why a stable cold and bare?
It's God's hand that placed Him there.
Why the angels all about?
It's the good news. Hear them shout!
Why the shepherds in that place?
They came to see His holy face.
Why the wise men from afar?
They've been guided by a star.
Why the child, asleep, I see?
Savior, King of kings, He'll be.

Are You Wise?
by Kenton K. Smith

How do you know if you are wise?
Must your brain be of greater-than-average size?
Must you read 300 books in a year,
And quote them to anyone willing to hear?
Must you earn for yourself a PhD
From a reputable university?
Must you use words of ponderous size,
Like *philanthropy* or *philosophize*?
Do you give up? Then here is a clue:
Wise men still seek Him—do you?

Wise Men

(a rhyme for three children)
by Dolores Steger

CHILD 1:   I am a wise man, and I have been told
A baby king's born. And I bring Him
    some gold.

       CHILD 2:   I am a wise man and, just for the king,
It's sweet-smelling incense that to Him
    I bring.

            CHILD 3:   I am a wise man and myrrh
    that's so mild
Is what I will give to that
    most special child.

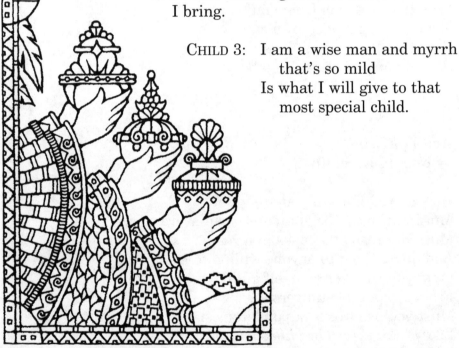

ALL: We are three wise men with gifts rare and new.
Will you, with all honor, bring gifts for Him too?

I Can Plainly See

(a verse for five children)
by Dolores Steger

CHILD 1:   I am just a little lamb,
But I can plainly see
A baby in a manger,
Lying nearby me.

CHILD 2:   I'm just a little donkey,
But I can plainly see
A Lord there in the manger,
Born to set men free.

CHILD 3:   I am just a little cow,
But I can plainly see
A prince there in the manger,
Sleeping peacefully.

CHILD 4:   I am just a little camel,
But I can plainly see
A king there in a manger.
A King of kings is He.

CHILD 5:   I am just a little dove,
But I can plainly see
A Savior in a manger
Who'll live eternally.

Four Questions of Christmas

by Phyllis Wezeman

Summary: A Christmas parallel to the Passover dinner in which four children ask questions about the significance of Jesus' birth.

Characters:
NARRATOR
FOUR CHILDREN

Setting: home that is being decorated on Christmas Eve

Props: decorated Christmas tree, extra ornaments to be put on tree, nativity scene, wrapped presents, bows to put on presents, stool for NARRATOR

Running Time: 5 minutes

[The NARRATOR sits on a stool off to one side with a separate spotlight. The FOUR CHILDREN are gathered around the tree. They can be placing ornaments on the tree, putting bows on presents and arranging them beneath the tree, or setting up the nativity scene.]

NARRATOR: Often traditions become so ingrained that families go through the motions of the holidays without stopping to think about the reasons behind seasonal celebrations. The Jewish religion understood the need to encourage examination of customs and traditions. The celebration of Passover, for example, would not be complete without the asking of the "four questions" that require the older generation to explain the reasons behind the ritual of the Seder meal to the youngest people present. Since Christmas is the celebration of the arrival of a baby to His Jewish parents, perhaps it would be appropriate to adopt this Jewish custom of asking questions in order to celebrate His birth.

CHILD ONE: On other days we go to church in the morning. Why on this night do we go to church so late?

NARRATOR: On Christmas Eve we remember that it was at night as the shepherds watched their sheep that the angels came to announce the birth of a special baby. The shepherds heard the angel chorus because they were awake and watching. On Christmas Eve we want to be awake and watching for the birth of Jesus too. So we share a special service with our friends at church to remember that Jesus, the Prince of Peace, was born in the gentle quiet of the night.

CHILD TWO: When it is someone's birthday, we usually take presents to the birthday girl or boy. Why on Jesus' birthday do we give presents to one another?

NARRATOR: On Jesus' birthday we give presents because the wise men took gifts of gold, frankincense, and myrrh to the baby Jesus. Jesus also taught us that the way to show our love for Him is to love one another. So on Christmas we share gifts, as the wise men did, but we share them with others in Jesus' name.

CHILD THREE: For no other holiday do we put up a tree inside the house. Why for this holiday do we bring a tree inside and put lights on it?

NARRATOR: Many years ago in Germany, the tradition of using a lighted tree at Christmas was begun. The green boughs of the evergreen tree symbolize for us that the gift Jesus brings is eternal life. The twinkling lights remind us that Jesus is the light of the world. The beauty of the lighted Christmas tree suggests the beauty of God's love for the world, a love that sent Jesus, God's only Son.

CHILD FOUR: At no other time do we set up a nativity scene. Why only at Christmas do we worship the baby in the manger?

NARRATOR: We worship God Almighty, the maker of the universe. Yet our human bodies cannot see or understand the power that God is. Because God wanted us to know how much we are loved, Jesus came as a baby, a human, just like us. The nativity scene reminds us of how God's love came to earth, love made known in Jesus, our Savior.

[Lights dim. All bow their heads as "Away in a Manger" or another appropriate Christmas song is sung.]

C-H-R-I-S-T-M-A-S Is . . .

by Mary Tucker

Summary: A presentation about Jesus' birth, using the letters in the word *Christmas*.

Characters:
NINE LETTER HOLDERS
THREE VERSE RECITERS
THREE ACTORS
CHILDREN'S CHORUS (to sing Christmas carols)

Props: nine large letter cards spelling *Christmas;* a large, gift-wrapped package (the top wrapped separately so it can be easily lifted off) with a word card inside that says, "Eternal Life"; a sign that says, "Tell everyone that Jesus is the Reason for the Season!"

Running Time: 15 minutes

Program Notes: If you have a limited number of children, you do not need a separate children's chorus. One child can play the parts of all three ACTORS. One child can read all the Bible verses.

For younger children, have children hold up each letter of *Christmas* as an older narrator reads each rhyme.

C H R

LETTER HOLDER ONE *[holds up letter C]:* Christmas is **carols** that we sing with joy, celebrating the birthday of God's little boy.

[CHILDREN'S CHORUS sings "Joy to the World."]

LETTER HOLDER TWO *[holds up letter H]:* Christmas is **hope** for the whole human race. Our hope is in Jesus who died in our place.

VERSE RECITER ONE: "We have put our hope in the living God, who is the Savior of all men, and especially of those who believe" (1 Timothy 4:10).

LETTER HOLDER THREE *[holds up letter R]:* Christmas is **receiving** the gift God gives—Jesus His Son—so that we may live.

ACTOR ONE *[holds up a gift-wrapped package and pretends to read label]:* From GOD *[points upward]* to YOU! *[points to audience; then opens package and removes card that says ETERNAL LIFE, holding it up for all to see]*

LETTER HOLDER FOUR *[holds up letter I]:* Christmas is **Immanuel**—the Son's special name that says God is with us! That's why He came.

[CHILDREN'S CHORUS sings "O Come, All Ye Faithful."]

LETTER HOLDER FIVE *[holds up letter S]:* Christmas is **shepherds** leaving their sheep to go see God's Son in a manger asleep.

I S T

VERSE RECITER TWO: "The shepherds returned, glorifying and praising God for all the things they had heard and seen" (Luke 2:20).

LETTER HOLDER SIX *[holds up letter T]:* Christmas is **telling** people we know that Jesus the Savior was born long ago. *[ACTOR TWO holds up a sign that says, "Tell everyone that Jesus is the Reason for the Season!"]*

LETTER HOLDER SEVEN *[holds up letter M]:* Christmas is a **manger** in a poor cattle stall. The baby who slept there is Lord of us all.

[CHILDREN'S CHORUS sings "Away in a Manger."]

LETTER HOLDER EIGHT *[holds up letter A]:* Christmas is **angels** filling the sky, praising the Lord on earth and on high.

ACTOR THREE *[waves arms overhead and shouts]:* Glory to God in the highest and on earth!

LETTER HOLDER NINE *[holds up letter S]:* Christmas is **special,** don't you agree? For Jesus, God's Son, came for you and for me!

VERSE RECITER THREE: "For God so loved the world that he gave his one and only Son, that whoever believes in him shall not perish but have eternal life" (John 3:16).

[CHILDREN'S CHORUS sings "Hark, The Herald Angels Sing."]

M A S

The Story of the Wise Men
by Phyllis Wezeman

Summary: A retelling of the story of the Magi in a dramatic way.

Characters:
NARRATOR
WISE MAN ONE
WISE MAN TWO
WISE MAN THREE
HEROD
PRIESTS (2 or more children)
CHIEF PRIEST

Setting: home that is being decorated on Christmas Eve

Props: copies of the script (optional props—see program notes)

Running Time: 10 minutes

Program Notes
This program is designed to be flexible both in presentation and in the number of children involved. Presentation will vary based on skills, preparation time, and performance needs. In Sunday school classes or worship services, a simple choral reading may be done with stools for actors and music stands to hold scripts, or readers may be scattered throughout the congregation and speak from the pews. A more elaborate production with costumes and memorized parts would make a meaningful seasonal program or devotion. Props needed for a dramatic production include Bible costumes for Herod, kings,

and priests; a large, decorated throne for Herod; wise men's gifts; a doll for the child Jesus; and a child to play the non-speaking character of Mary.

To involve more children, create larger acting groups to represent the wise men and priests.

No matter the level of presentation, participants should be encouraged to practice the script aloud several times and to rehearse when to stand and speak. Readers should be reminded to breathe deeply and project voices, to read with feeling, slowly and distinctly.

NARRATOR *[facing congregation]:* Now when Jesus was born in Bethlehem of Judea in the days of Herod the King *[HEROD stands, smiles, and gestures in a kingly way.],* behold, wise men from the east came to Jerusalem *[three WISE MEN stand]* saying,

WISE MAN ONE: Where is He who has been born king of the Jews?

WISE MAN TWO: For we have seen His star in the east,

WISE MAN THREE: And have come to worship Him.
[All bow from the waist.]

The Story of the Wise Men

NARRATOR: When Herod the king heard this, he was troubled *[HEROD stands, growls, and complains.]* and all Jerusalem with him. *[PRIESTS growl and complain.]* And assembling all the chief priests and scribes of the people *[PRIESTS stand.],* he inquired of them:

HEROD: Where is the Christ supposed to be born?

PRIESTS: In Bethlehem of Judea, for so it is written by the prophet:

CHIEF PRIEST: And you, O Bethlehem, in the land of Judah, are by no means least among the rulers of Judah; for from you shall come a ruler who will govern my people Israel.

NARRATOR: Then Herod summoned the wise men secretly and ascertained from them what time the star appeared. *[HEROD gestures and WISE MEN turn toward HEROD.]* And he sent them to Bethlehem, saying:

HEROD *[insincerely]:* Go and search diligently for the child, and when you have found him, bring me word, that I too may come and worship him *[WISE MEN bow and nod agreement.]*

NARRATOR: When they had heard the king, they went their way. *[HEROD and PRIESTS sit.]*

WISE MEN: Let's go! Follow that star! There it goes!

NARRATOR: And lo, the star which they had seen in the east went before them, till it came to rest over the place where the child was.

WISE MAN ONE: In that stable???

NARRATOR: When they saw the star, they rejoiced exceedingly!

WISE MEN *[quietly]:* Yay!

NARRATOR: And going into the house, they saw the child with Mary his mother, and they fell down and worshiped him. *[WISE MEN bow, or kneel, and look worshipful.]* Then, opening their treasures, they offered Him gifts.

WISE MAN ONE: Gold!

WISE MAN TWO: Frankincense!

WISE MAN THREE: And myrrh!

NARRATOR: And being warned in a dream not to return to Herod *[WISE MEN make a "sh-h-h-h!" sign and pretend to tiptoe away as HEROD stands.],* they departed to their own country by another way. *[WISE MEN sit as HEROD looks around, and then shrugs and sits.]*

NARRATOR: And so ends our lesson of the visit of the wise men. Let those who are wise still listen to the angels' voices and follow the light of the Bethlehem star! *[NARRATOR sits.]*

The First Christmas

by Alyce Pickett

Summary: A short retelling of the Christmas story using rhyme.

Characters:
JOSEPH
MARY
ANGELS
SHEPHERDS
MAGI
STAR
NARRATOR
CHILDREN'S CHOIR

Props: large, printed name cards on string to go around the neck of each character; costumes for characters, such as angels' robes, shepherd's staffs, a glittery poster board star (all optional)

[The characters may line up in groups in order. Each group may step forward when it is their turn to speak.]

JOSEPH: Mary and I came a long, long way
And reached Bethlehem late one day;
So late we could find no room at all.
We rested that night in a cattle stall.

MARY: That night I welcomed my baby son,
Little Lord Jesus, the holy one.
For God had chosen me to be
The mother of the Christ-baby.

[CHILDREN'S CHOIR sings "O Little Town of Bethlehem."]

ANGELS: That night God sent us down to earth
With the good news of Jesus' birth.
Rejoicing, we sang praises, and then
We went back to Heaven again.

SHEPHERDS: Outside Bethlehem that dark night
We saw heavenly angels bright
And heard the news they came to
    bring
About the little Christ-child king.

[CHILDREN'S CHOIR sings "Silent Night."]

MAGI: We saw the new star appear
And knew God's promised one was
    here.
We traveled far our gifts to bring
To this little Christ-child king.

STAR: The Magi rested every day;
Then I helped them find their way.
High in the sky, shining bright,
I guided them throughout the night.

[CHILDREN'S CHOIR sings "We Three Kings of Orient Are."]

NARRATOR: Remember now that wonderful night.
Worship again the Lord of light.
Together now our praises bring
To Lord and Savior, risen king!

[CHILDREN'S CHOIR sings "Joy to the World."]

A Christmas to Remember

Summary: A simple acting out of the Christmas story with a backdrop of Scripture for preschool and young elementary children

Characters:
NARRATOR
ANGELS
MARY
JOSEPH
DECREE HOLDER
DONKEY
SHEPHERDS
SHEEP
STAR HOLDER
WISE MEN

Props: Bible costumes for MARY and JOSEPH, a manger with hay, a doll for baby Jesus, ears for SHEEP and the DONKEY, white robes for ANGELS, a scroll-like, official-looking paper for Caesar's decree, a recorded sound of a donkey's *hee haw* (if possible), staffs for SHEPHERDS, a glittery star attached to a dowel or ruler to hold high in the air, an older-looking doll for toddler Jesus, gifts for WISE MEN, two large painted poster board backdrops—a desert with a palm tree and a stable (optional)

Running Time: 10-15 minutes

Program Notes: This program can be done with almost any number of children and is very simple to organize and practice. There are no actual speaking parts for children to memorize, only actions. Older children can be assigned the parts of MARY, JOSEPH, and the WISE MEN. The NARRATOR should be an adult, and you will need several adults sitting in front to cue children at the appropriate times.

[The desert backdrop should be set up stage left and the stable backdrop with the manger in front of it stage right. The children may stand in groups in the center of the stage. An ANGEL and MARY should be stage left.]

NARRATOR: Over 2,000 years ago, God sent the angel Gabriel to Nazareth, a town in Galilee, to a woman named Mary who was pledged to be married to a man named Joseph. *[MARY kneels before the ANGEL in fear. The ANGEL places his hand on MARY'S shoulder to comfort her.]* The angel said, "Do not be afraid, Mary. You have found favor with God. You will be with child and give birth to a Son, and you are to give Him the name Jesus."

   [MARY nods her head up and down in agreement.] "I am the Lord's servant," Mary answered. "May it be to me as you have said." Then the angel left her. *[The ANGEL leaves.]*

[JOSEPH joins MARY on the stage left.]

NARRATOR: In those days, Caesar Augustus issued a decree that a census should be taken of the entire Roman world. *[DECREE HOLDER walks across stage in front of JOSEPH and MARY holding his decree in front of him and pretending to read loudly from it.]*

Joseph also went up from the town of Nazareth in Galilee to Bethlehem, the town of David, because he belonged to the house and line of David. *[DONKEY moves in a* hee haw *motion across stage as prompted by recorded* hee haw *sounds. JOSEPH and MARY follow DONKEY across stage.]* He went there to register with Mary, who was pledged to be married to him and was expecting a child. *[JOSEPH puts his arm around MARY and smiles widely.]* But there was no room for them in the Bethlehem inn, so they stayed in a stable. *[JOSEPH and MARY shrug and settle in on either side of manger.]* While they were there, the time came for Mary's baby to be born. She had her firstborn, a Son, and she wrapped Him in cloths and laid Him in a manger. *[Adult hands MARY baby Jesus and she cuddles Him and lays Him in the manger.]*

[SHEPHERDS move to stage left.]

NARRATOR: And there were shepherds living out in the fields nearby, keeping watch over their flocks at night. *[SHEEP baa several times.]* An angel of the Lord appeared to them, and they were terrified. *[ANGEL moves to stage left and pretends to speak to SHEPHERDS as they fall to the ground in fear.]* But the angel said, "Do not be afraid. I bring you good news of great joy that will be for all the people. Today in the town of David a Savior has been born to you; He is Christ the Lord. This will be a sign to you: You will find a baby wrapped in clothes and lying in a manger."

Suddenly a great company of the heavenly host appeared with the angel, praising God and saying *[Other ANGELS turn and face SHEPHERDS and wave arms and pretend to sing.]*, "Glory to God in the highest, and on earth peace to men on whom His favor rests."

A Christmas to Remember

[ANGELS leave. SHEPHERDS get up and look at each other and gesture excitedly. SHEEP baa.]

NARRATOR: When the angels had left them and gone into Heaven, the shepherds said to one another. "Let's go to Bethlehem and see this thing that has happened, which the Lord has told us about." *[SHEPHERDS walk across stage and bow in front of manger.]* So they hurried off and found Mary and Joseph, and the baby, who was lying in the manger.

[SHEPHERDS return to center group. WISE MEN move stage left. Stage right, remove manger and set up a chair for MARY to sit in with JOSEPH behind her, an older doll in her lap.]

NARRATOR: After Jesus was born in Bethlehem in Judea, during the time of King Herod, Wise Men from the east saw a star in the east. They knew that a king had been born and came to worship Him. *[STAR HOLDER holds up star in air, and WISE MEN follow it across the stage to where Jesus is.]* On coming to the house, they saw the child with His mother, Mary, and they bowed down and worshiped Him. *[WISE MEN bow before Jesus and present their gifts one at a time, as the narrator says them.]* Then they presented Him with gifts of gold and of incense and of myrrh.

[MARY, JOSEPH, and WISE MEN, rise and move to center stage.]

NARRATOR: And so Mary and Joseph *[Each group bows their head when the narrator mentions them. The DECREE and STAR HOLDER may bow their heads with the WISE MEN.]*, the angels, the shepherds with their sheep, and the wise men all worshiped and welcomed Jesus, God's only Son.

Christmas Celebration of Love
by Carolyn R. Scheidies

Summary: A choral and dramatic program for preschool through 6th grade.

Characters:
NARRATOR 1
NARRATOR 2
MARY, JOSEPH, SHEPHERDS (non-speaking parts)
GRADES 5 AND 6
GRADES 1 AND 2
GRADES 3 AND 4
PRESCHOOL

Props: baby doll; manger; cross in background; Bible costumes for MARY, JOSEPH, SHEPHERDS; decorated Christmas tree; tinsel; wrapped gifts

Running Time: 45 minutes

Program Notes: This program can be adapted to almost any number of children. Songs are suggestions only. Substitute your children's favorite Christmas songs about Jesus.
When the program refers to ALL singing, the congregation may join in with the children.

[GRADES 1–6 are lined up on stage left. NARRATORS are stage right in front of a Christmas tree with lights and presents. The manger scene is in the center of the stage. A spotlight focuses on NARRATOR 1 as he begins to speak.]

NARRATOR 1: "But you, Bethlehem Ephrathah, though you are small among the clans of Judah, out of you will come for me one who will be ruler over Israel, whose origins are from of old, from ancient times" (Micah 5:2).

[ALL sing "Joy to the World."]

NARRATOR 1: "In those days Caesar Augustus issued a decree that a census should be taken of the entire Roman world. (This was the first census that took place while Quirinius was governor of Syria.) And everyone went to his own town to register. So Joseph also went up from the town of Nazareth in Galilee to Judea, to Bethlehem the town of David, because he belonged to the house and line of David" (Luke 2:1-4).

NARRATOR 2: "He went there to register with Mary, who was pledged to be married to him and was expecting a child. While they were there, the time came for the baby to be born, and she gave birth to her firstborn, a son. She wrapped him in cloths and placed him in a manger, because there was no room for them in the inn" (Luke 2:5-7).

[ALL sing "O Little Town of Bethlehem."
As they sing, MARY and JOSEPH come
down the aisle and onto center stage
where MARY kneels by the manger
as JOSEPH stands beside her.]

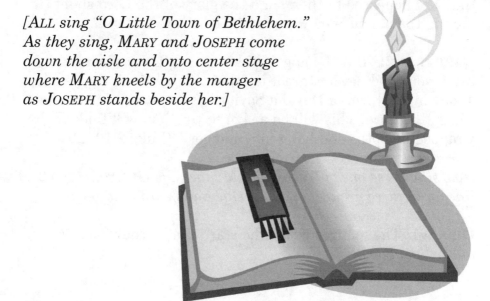

GRADES 5 AND 6: Christmas comes but once a year,

GRADES 1 AND 2: A time of joy and celebration.

GRADES 3 AND 4: But Jesus didn't come to make a splash,

ALL: He came to bring humankind salvation.

[ALL sing "O Come, All Ye Faithful" as PRESCHOOL lines up on stage.]

PRESCHOOL: I may be small,
But this I know is true,
Jesus came to earth because
He loves me *[point to self]* and you *[point to audience]*.

[ALL sing "O Come, Let Us Adore Him" as PRESCHOOL returns to sit with their parents.]

NARRATOR 1: "And there were shepherds living out in the fields nearby, keeping watch over their flocks at night. An angel of the Lord appeared to them, and the glory of the Lord shone around them, and they were terrified" (Luke 2:8, 9).

NARRATOR 2: "But the angel said to them, 'Do not be afraid. I bring you good news of great joy that will be for all the people. Today in the town of David a Savior has been born to you; he is Christ the Lord. This will be a sign to you: You will find a baby wrapped in cloths and lying in a manger'" (Luke 2:10-12).

[ALL sing verse one of "Away in a Manger" as GRADES 1 AND 2 line up in three groups on either side and behind manger.]

GROUP 1: The manger is but the start of a journey *[motion toward manger]*,

GROUP 2: That continued to the cross *[motion toward cross behind manger]*

GROUP 3: Where Jesus sacrificed His life *[arms crossed on chest, heads bowed]*

ALL GRADES 1 AND 2: But, oh, how great the cost.

[ALL sing verse two of "Away in a Manger" as GRADES 1 AND 2 return to choral group.]

NARRATOR 2: "Suddenly a great company of the heavenly host appeared with the angel, praising God and saying, 'Glory to God in the highest, and on earth peace to men on whom his favor rests'" (Luke 2:13, 14).

[ALL sing "Angels from the Realms of Glory" while SHEPHERDS come down the aisle, go up on stage, and kneel in front of the manger. GRADES 3 AND 4 move to the front of the group.]

GRADES 3 AND 4: He didn't leave His glory

SOLO CHILD: For tinsel, gifts, and trees. *[If church is decorated with a tree, indicate it.]*

SOLO CHILD: He came to offer forgiveness and hope *[hand over heart]*,

GRADES 3 AND 4: And to set His people free *[arms out]*.

NARRATOR 2: "The Spirit of the Sovereign LORD is on me, because the LORD has anointed me to preach good news to the poor. He has sent me to bind up the brokenhearted, to proclaim freedom for the captives and release from darkness for the prisoners" (Isaiah 61:1).

GRADES 3 AND 4: Dying on the cross He showed

SOLO CHILD: A love so great and true. *[form heart in the air]*

SOLO CHILD: He died and yet He rose again, *[raise hands, palm up, from knees to above shoulders]*

GRADES 3 AND 4: All for me and you. *[indicate self, audience]*

[ALL sing "Hark! The Herald Angels Sing" while GRADES 3 AND 4 return to their places. GRADES 5 AND 6 move forward and make two semicircles on either side of the manger scene.]

NARRATOR 1: "The LORD has done great things for us, and we are filled with joy" (Psalm 126:3).

SEMICIRCLE 1: In the business of the season,

SEMICIRCLE 2: Let us not forget the one

SEMICIRCLE 1: Whose birthday that we celebrate

GRADES 5 AND 6: God's one and only Son.

NARRATOR 1: "The people walking in darkness have seen a great light; on those living in the land of the shadow of death a light has dawned" (Isaiah 9:2).

NARRATOR 2: "For God did not send his Son into the world to condemn the world, but to save the world through him" (John 3:17).

[ALL sing "God Sent His Son" to the tune "God Is So Good."]

SEMICIRCLE 1: Let us not forget the cross *[spotlight on cross in background]* shadows the manger scene *[spotlight on manger],*

SEMICIRCLE 2: For the gift He gave was the gift of life He offers you and me.

NARRATOR 2: "For God so loved the world that he gave his one and only Son, that whoever believes in him shall not perish but have eternal life" (John 3:16).

NARRATOR 1: Christmas comes but once a year *[kneels before manger],*

NARRATOR 2: Oh, what a celebration *[kneels before manger].*

ALL CHILDREN: As today we bow before our Lord *[bow heads and face manger]*

ALL: To accept His great salvation.

[ALL sing "Joy to the World."]

Christmas Celebration of Love

Witness to the World

An Advent Celebration
by Phyllis Wezeman and Ann Liechty

Summary: A unique look at the Advent season that uses as its theme celebrations around the world. The program may be performed in its entirety at the beginning of Advent to explain its significance to families. Or the five segments may be divided between the weeks of Advent.

Characters:

FIVE FAMILIES

SIX OLDER CHILDREN TO PERFORM FIRST PERSON DRAMAS (if possible, children from each of the five families)

Props: an Advent wreath with five candles, matches or a lighter, Bible, wooden manger for the offering time, candles for each member of the audience

Program Notes: Different family members can be assigned to read Scripture, read the Commentary, and light the candle. If possible, an older child in the family can perform the first-person drama. You may choose to provide costumes for each of the dramas.

Candle One: Serving

Scripture Reading: Mark 13:26-37

First Person Drama: Andrew
My name is Andrew. Today marks the beginning of the season of Advent, a time of waiting. Being a fisherman and a disciple, I know the importance of learning to wait—whether you're waiting for the nets to fill with fish or waiting for God to supply a miracle to feed a hungry crowd. Those of us who follow Jesus are called to wait expectantly: to offer God our time of waiting and watching by being open to serving others.

Commentary: On the first Sunday in Advent, we remember that Christians around the world are called to serve others as they wait for Christ's birth.

Saint Andrew's Day, celebrated on November 30 in many places around the world, reminds us of the witness of Andrew, the disciple who served Jesus by serving others. It was Andrew who brought many to Jesus, including a small boy with five loaves and two fish that fed 5,000 people. Andrew's example challenges us to spend our days of waiting for Christmas by serving others. God can make a big difference even with our small beginnings.

[Light the first Advent candle.]

Song: "O Come, O Come, Emmanuel"

Candle Two: Surprising

Scripture Reading: Luke 1:46-55

First Person Drama: Saint Nicholas
My name is Nicholas. Perhaps you know me as Saint Nicholas. Perhaps it would surprise you to know that I lived my life for Christ and His church. I enjoyed giving presents to those in need. As you wait during Advent, perhaps you will be inspired as I was to pass along the joy and delight of Christmas. The beautiful surprises of Christmastime are meant only to remind us of the surprising gift of God—a Son born in a lowly stable who now reigns in the glory of Heaven with all the saints.

Commentary: On the second Sunday in Advent, we remembered that Christians around the world are challenged to share the surprising news of God's love.

Saint Nicholas Day, celebrated on December 6 in many places around the world, reminds us of the witness of Nicholas, who used his wealth to help others. Nicholas gave away his money and shared gifts with others because he knew God's surprising gift of love in his own life. His example challenged us to spend our days waiting for Christmas by sharing God's surprising love with others. Everyone loves surprises. The biggest surprise of all is how much more we receive by giving.

[Light the second Advent candle.]

Song: "Come, Thou Long Expected Jesus"

Candle Three: Shining

Scripture Reading: John 1:6-8, 19-28

First Person Drama: Santa Lucia

My name is Lucy. Maybe you have heard my name pronounced *Lucia*. Both *Lucia* and *Lucy* are from the Latin word for *light*. In my life I chose to follow the light of Christ, even accepting death before I would betray my faith in Jesus.

I am honored that my name is remembered and used during the season of Advent, a time when we prepare for the coming of the true light of the world. May Christ's light keep shining through each of us as we prepare for His rebirth this Christmas.

Commentary: On the third Sunday of Advent, we remember that Christians around the world help prepare the way for Christ by letting the light of faith shine through their words and deeds.

Santa Lucia Day, December 13, is celebrated around the world as a festival of light, helping prepare for the birth of the true light of the world at Christmas. Lucia was a young woman who gave away everything she had, even the money for her wedding, to help the poor and needy. She refused to give up her faith in Christ even when she was threatened with death. In many places around the world, her kindness and bravery are celebrated with festivals that feature a young girl wearing a crown made of a wreath with candles. Lucia's example reminds us to let our faith shine out to the world so that others may find their way to the Christ child.

[Light the third Advent candle.]

Song: "O Little Town Of Bethlehem"

Candle Four: Seeking

Scripture Reading: Luke 2:1-7

First Person Drama: Innkeeper

I am the innkeeper, famous because I once told a young couple from Nazareth that I had no room in my inn for them to sleep. I know you think it seemed cruel of me to turn them away, but I was not a seeker of anything but money then. I was not about to put out a paying guest to house some poor peasants. But she looked so trusting, and their baby was due so soon. What was I to do? That is the question each of us must answer in this season of seeking called Advent. This is my witness to you. I made a place for Him to be born, first in my stable and then in my heart. How about you? Will you make room?

Commentary: On the fourth Sunday in Advent we remember that just as Mary and Joseph sought God's provisions through the help of an innkeeper, Christians must also seek and trust God to use their lives as a witness to the power of His love in the world.

The Mexican Posada festival occurs for nine days from December 16 to December 24. During this time whole communities gather to reenact the journey of Mary and Joseph, who once sought shelter for the birth of Jesus. The pilgrims who knock and the innkeepers who turn them away remind us that we have a choice to make in Advent. We too must open our hearts and welcome the Christ child.

[Light the fourth Advent candle.]

Song: "O Come, All Ye Faithful"

Candle Five: Saving

Scripture Reading: Luke 2:1-20

First Person Drama: Joseph and Mary

JOSEPH: My name is Joseph; this is my wife, Mary. We understand that the whole world celebrates with us on December 25, Jesus' birthday. Jesus delighted us from the first moment we saw Him.

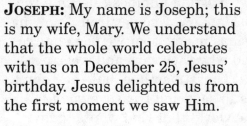

MARY: Joseph and I saved many memories of Jesus' childhood, as most parents do. However, even more important than our saving of memories is the truth that Jesus came to save the world.

JOSEPH: Just as a parent treasures a child, God treasures each one of us. So today, Jesus' birthday is a celebration of hope, not only for us but for the world.

Commentary: On Christmas Day we remember that the newborn Jesus brought the gift of saving love, not only to His family but also to the world.

December 25 marks the day celebrated around the world as the birthday of Jesus. On this day Christian families celebrate that God sent Jesus to save the world. Our joy comes from knowing that the gift of Jesus at Christmas means that we need not be lost. People seem to understand why they save and treasure the gifts and memories made at Christmastime, but they don't all understand that God wants to save and treasure *them*. Christians must share with the world that God wants to give everyone eternal life, and the way to understand and receive that gift is through God's Son, Jesus.

[Light the Christ candle.]

Song: "Joy to the World"

Offering: Receive an offering for a special cause or mission project. Place a wooden manger at the front of the sanctuary and invite worshipers to come forward to place their gifts, symbolic of offering themselves to the Christ child.

Closing Song: "Silent Night"

[As the song begins, the worship leader lights a candle from the Christ candle and in turn lights the candles of the ushers, who then take the light to the first person in each pew. Each person, in turn, "passes the light" to his or her neighbor.]

Giving Thanks

By Alyce Pickett

Summary: A poem of thanks to God written for five children.

ALL: We want to tell the Lord above
That we are thankful for His love.

CHILD ONE: I thank God for my family
And all the things He does for me.

CHILD TWO: For God's care and parents who
Love and care about me too.

CHILD THREE: I'm thankful for Jesus and that He
Always watches over me.

CHILD FOUR: For home and all my loved ones
there,
For school and friends and toys to
share.

CHILD FIVE: For family, food, pets, and play
And that God loves me every day.

ALL: We thank You, Lord, for our free
land
And every blessing from Your hand.

A Thanksgiving Feast

by Christine Spence

I fold my hands and bow my head
and close my eyes while prayer is said.
The dog is sniffing by my chair.
I wonder if the food's still there.
I think I'll open just one eye
So I can check the pumpkin pie.

All eyes are closed. Oh this is fun!
I can look at everyone!
Thank You, God, for giving me
All those in my family—
Grandpa, Grandma, Father, Mother,
Little sister, baby brother.
Thank You, God. You love me too
And sent me Jesus. I love You.